Sounds

...and 51 More Poems in Villanelle Form

(Fine . . . but what's a Villanelle? See page 1.)

David Crump

Gotham Books

30 N Gould St.
Ste. 20820, Sheridan, WY 82801
https://gothambooksinc.com/

Phone: 1 (307) 464-7800

© 2024 *David Crump*. All rights reserved.

No part of this book may be reproduced, stored in a retrieval system, or transmitted by any means without the written permission of the author.

Published by Gotham Books (April 23, 2024)

ISBN: 979-8-88775-884-8 (P)
ISBN: 979-8-88775-885-5 (E)

Because of the dynamic nature of the Internet, any web addresses or links contained in this book may have changed since publication and may no longer be valid.

The views expressed in this work are solely those of the author and do not necessarily reflect the views of the publisher, and the publisher hereby disclaims any responsibility for them.

To Susanne

. . . with thanks to Amanda
I couldn't have done it without you

Contents

So, What's a Villanelle? 1
MY LOVE 3
EASY STREET 4
SOUNDS 5
SCIENTIFIC METHOD 6
AN OLD MAN LOOKS OUTSIDE 7
Why 52 Villanelles? 9
INFLATION 10
JOHNNY RAY 11
LUBBOCK, TEXAS 12
TWELVE MONTH VILLANELLE 13
THE WRITER DRILLS HIS BRAIN 14
DOUBLE DIAMOND RANCH, WYOMING 15
VICIOUS DUMB CRIMINALS 16
PHYSICAL THERAPY 17
MOVING DAY 18
SILLY SAM: HERE'S ONE FOR THE KIDS 19
THE GOOD AND THE BAD DONALD TRUMP 20
DEATH ROW FABLES 21
Great Villanelles of the Past 23
NEW HOME PURCHASE 24
THE ISLAMIC REPUBLIC OF IRAN 25
ANDERSON STREET VILLANELLE 26
EMAILS 27

SENTINEL	28
WORLD SERIES 2022: THE HOUSTON POINT OF VIEW	29
WAKING UP AT FOUR A.M.	30
AUSTIN, TEXAS	31
EDGAR ALLAN POE	32
SHOPGIRL	33
CROSSWORD PUZZLES	34
A YELLOW WOOD AND BAD ADVICE	37
A QUEEN FOR AMERICA	38
GRAB THE DAY	39
A VILLANELLE SHOVED TOGETHER OUT OF SEVERAL REALLY OLD AND TIRED JOKES	40
THE XANADU DOME	41
ELVIS	42
NEW HOUSTON VISITOR	43
COVID	44
ALWAYS, FOREVER REAL	45
RETIRE? BUT WHAT WILL YOU DO?	46
SEMIOTICS, METAPHYSICS, AND THE COLOR CALLED "RED"	47
DOGS	48
TRUTH	49
CARGO FROM HOUSTON	50
LAKE HOUSE	51
YEAR'S END, 2022	52
FIRST GRADER	53
FORM 1040	54
LOSING	55

GRADUATE SCHOOL PROFESSORS 56
YOUR WEATHERMAN, NEHEMIAH GREENE 57
PENELOPE WAITS FOR ODYSSEUS 58
SAILING INTO HEADWINDS 59
WORDS 60

So, What's a Villanelle?

A villanelle has 19 required lines. The first five stanzas are 3 lines each, all rhymed in a fixed way (ABA). The last stanza is 4 lines, also with fixed rhymes.

Every line must be in "iambic pentameter," meaning five da-DUM beats. An unexpected example appears in the Rolling Stones' song *Honky-Tonk Women:* "I **met** a **gin**-soaked **bar**-room **queen** in **Mem**-phis." Perfect iambic pentameter.

So, villanelles are difficult to write. The first and third lines alternate to end each of the next four stanzas. These two lines are also the final lines. They've got to be good.

The rules aren't absolute. There can also be three-syllable beats called dactyls (da-da-DUM). The rhyme scheme can vary. But still, a villanelle is tricky.

So, here are my own villanelles. The subjects are varied. *Easy Street,* the second one, is just fun, with no message. Many are like that. But some are deeper.

MY LOVE

She's always more beautiful every year that goes by,
But she doesn't believe me whenever I tell her so.
She shows how she loves me without even having to try.

We met in summer, with heat as bold as July.
As the song should have said, she had me before hello.
She's always more beautiful every year that goes by.

Her singular, elegant eyes were reasons why
I found myself staring. Just one of the reasons, though.
She shows how she loves me without even having to try.

My woman, I'll love you until the moment I die,
But you and I have a lot more living to do.
You're always more beautiful every year that goes by.

Through trouble and cheer, but at times not eye to eye,
And not without skirmishes, always together we go.
You show how you love me without even having to try.

I'm sure I'll repeat this, all in a peaceful glow,
As time sends trials, the wearisome weathers that blow:
"You're always more beautiful every year that goes by,
"And you show how you love me without even having to try."

EASY STREET

In the vision of Easy Street that I have seen,
There are walls in front of mansions approaching the sky,
And lawns that are mowed and clipped and always green.

The women wear designer. They never cook or clean.
The men, in chalk-striped suits, just sell and buy,
In the vision of Easy Street that I have seen.

Their children, in wondrous wagons, wildly careen,
But the parents, at leisure, protect with a satisfied eye.
Their lawns are mowed and clipped and always green.

The folks there drink champagne in the limousine,
Play tennis on the weatherproof court behind the lanai,
In the vision of Easy Street that I have seen.

Their acreage features trees that never lean
And roses red forever, attendants nearby;
And lawns that are mowed and clipped and always green.

On Easy Street, no one's angry or mean
And rules that hinder others don't apply.
This is the vision of Easy Street that I have seen:
The lawns are mowed and clipped and always green.

SOUNDS

It's only a bucket of sound. Does it sound sort of good?
It's only a cluster of rhymes. Does it couple them well?
It's only words. Do they do whatever they should?

A verse has a shape, not a lesson. I guess it could,
Perhaps, discover its patterns with stories to tell,
But it's only a bucket of sound. Does it sound sort of good?

A message comes from statues made of wood,
Or bronze, or marble: let pride in legends swell,
But a poem is only words. Do they do what they should?

It's ronly bonly syllables, letters that flood
The floor with repeated pulses like strokes from a bell,
But it's only a bucket of sound. Does it sound sort of good?

After it ends, does it stand where it always stood,
Or maybe it rattles your rhythm for just a spell?
It's only words. Do they do whatever they should?

The beats and measures, falling wherever they fell,
They ought to stir you more than the wind in a well,
But it's only a bucket of sound. Does it sound sort of good?
It's only words. Do they do whatever they should?

SCIENTIFIC METHOD

Apollo's transport told the sun to shine,
The Romans said. And that's how the day was created.
This was the vision the oracles saw at the time.

Ptolemy stationed earth at the center, and spheres that aligned
Made music, they said, when stars grew bright, then faded.
Did Apollo's transport tell the sun to shine?

They convicted Galileo. His blasphemous crime
Was telling the Pope that the planet circulated,
Which wasn't the vision the oracles saw at the time.

Then Kepler showed us that orbits were ovals. His hardy design
Relied on the movement of Mars, which retrograded.
Did Apollo's transport tell the sun to shine?

Our star will become a Red Giant, prophets opine,
In five billion years, engulfing the earth unabated.
This is the vision the oracles see in our time.

Not even the law of gravity sits in a shrine.
Beliefs are false when the measurement can't be repeated.
Apollo's transport told the sun to shine,
And that was the vision the oracles saw at the time.

AN OLD MAN LOOKS OUTSIDE

An old man looks outside and hopes to see
The world and maybe a passing bird or two.
He wishes he could become what he wants to be.

He's lost a thousand intentions that once were free.
His choices were enemies, killing what could've been true.
An old man looks outside and hopes to see.

He's lost the desire to cut and split a tree.
He's lost the desire to game some foolish taboo.
He wishes he could become what he wants to be.

He wants to reclaim his longtime buckled knee.
He wants to reclaim the love that once he knew.
An old man looks outside and hopes to see.

He's gone from the ways he walked and that distant decree
To rescue the chances that earlier visions grew.
He wishes he could become what he wants to be.

He's almost seventy, searching in sturdy degree
To turn up the fire and try what he used to do.
An old man looks outside and hopes to see:
He wishes he could become what he wants to be.

Why 52 Villanelles?

Because I tried to do one a week for a year.

Writing takes discipline. There's nothing like a fixed schedule to make you disciplined.

And to keep that discipline going, there's nothing like having a whole bunch of people watching you. So, I put together an email list of family and friends and announced that I was going to send them a villanelle a week for 52 weeks,

I got some help along the way. My friend Donald Mace Williams really helped (he's the author of ***Wolfe***, a wonderful wild west epic that retells the *Beowulf* story). He gave me welcome advice about everything from meter to surplusage. Also, Bert Graham and Tommy Fibich gave me suggestions and feedback. Any deficiencies are mine alone, of course.

A funny thing about writing: if you get started, it flows. And after seventeen weeks, I had more than 52. So, here's the book.

INFLATION

Stealthy, like the touch of a cruel contagion,
Slow, like the fog, so that no one knows it's near,
Inflation fools us, and soon it's a conflagration.

The Federal Reserve? Those governors' inspiration
Tells them to bump the rate, but results aren't clear.
It's stealthy, like the touch of a cruel contagion.

Congress senses the oncoming polarization.
Let's pass an "Inflation Reduction Act!" But the name's not sincere.
Inflation fools us, and soon it's a conflagration.

The crowd at the pumps of the corner gasoline station?
Unaffordable food is the true disaster they fear.
It's stealthy, like the touch of a cruel contagion.

A tiny drop, and the President brags to the nation.
It's still a tax on the needy, and still, it's here.
Inflation fools us, and soon it's a conflagration.

Everyone wants it down, but dimming its flare
Depends on buyers and sellers everywhere.
It's stealthy, like the touch of a cruel contagion.
Inflation fools us, and soon it's a conflagration.

JOHNNY RAY

This friend of mine whose name is Johnny Ray,
You go to see him, winter, spring, or fall,
You'll find him drunk most any time of day.

He gulps that whiskey down. He'll never stray
From a hundred proof in bourbon, not at all,
This friend of mine whose name is Johnny Ray.

He drains it clean, like after a rum array,
Tequila that forces anyone else to sprawl.
You'll find him drunk most any time of day.

Beer and wine, now those he puts away
Like a yeoman sailor at least a yardarm tall,
This friend of mine whose name is Johnny Ray.

He sobered up just briefly, end of May,
For three or so sunsets, then headed out to the mall,
And you'll find him drunk most any time of day.

He won the lottery, got some princely pay.
"So why should I work? Or answer anyone's call?"
This friend of mine whose name is Johnny Ray,
You'll find him drunk most any time of day.

LUBBOCK, TEXAS

The wind of winter turns streets into wandering snow,
And summer burns so that birds don't want to sing.
Still, it's a town that a few brave tourists know.

It's got some pretty regions where wine grapes grow
And spots with harlequin flowers in gracious spring,
But the wind of winter turns streets into wandering snow.

Pointed galoshes for boots with pointed toes
Are what you need, and a colorful hatband ring.
This is a town that a few brave tourists know.

Downtown, a sand pit has prairie dogs below,
And the Buddy Holly* building is crammed with the Crickets' things,
But the wind of winter turns streets into wandering snow.

There's a big university, filled with classes in rows,
From ancient Greek to cosmic theories of string,
But still, it's a town that a few brave tourists know.

Students drive the Loop for a Saturday fling.
They watch the football team and its double wing.
The wind of winter turns streets into wandering snow,
But still, it's a town that a few brave tourists know.

---

*Buddy Holly and the Crickets did wonderful songs, like "That'll Be the Day" and "True Love Ways."

TWELVE MONTH VILLANELLE

Sometimes the change is fun. But sometimes not.
December, for instance, has Christmas, but mostly it's cold.
Some of the seasons, sadly, are way too hot.

Come January, the old year's mistakes are a blot.
In February, winter has its hold,
So sometimes the change is fun. But sometimes not.

March has warmth, but only some, not a lot.
April is spring, but it's mostly oversold.
Some of the seasons, sadly, are way too hot.

May has weather that really hits the spot.
Then June begins the summer, so I'm told,
And sometimes the change is fun. But sometimes not.

July has the Fourth, but that isn't all it's got:
Like August, it's sizzling and humid. The summer gets old,
And these two months, sadly, are way too hot.

September opens the schools, and leaves get rolled.
October's like May. The weather's perfect gold.
November's my birthday. An extra line for the slot.
Sometimes the change is fun. But sometimes not.
Some of the seasons, sadly, are way too hot.

THE WRITER DRILLS HIS BRAIN

It's easy. You only drill around in your brain
With an image and rotate it hard. It's self-defeating:
A weary journey, a battle for little gain.

You write so the words are strung in a simple chain,
But the effortless talk you've sounded makes boring reading.
It's easy. You only drill around in your brain.

You try to make the meaning sharp and plain
But then it's excessively plain, with too much repeating.
A weary journey, a battle for little gain.

You punch the computer, and half goes down the drain.
Whatever you offer, that silly machine is eating.
It's easy. You only drill around in your brain.

It's almost finished, but now you can't maintain
The message with what you wrote that was just preceding:
A weary journey, a battle for little gain.

And then, there's a breakthrough. A line as right as rain
Can make it fun, a line with powerful meaning.
It's easy. You only drilled around in your brain:
A journey, a battle, and now there's plenty of gain.

DOUBLE DIAMOND RANCH, WYOMING

We still have cowboys. Maybe the best of the breed.
They cuss about thunderstorms, riding the endless lines.
Remember the day when the land had a simpler creed?

Tractors can sling that Coastal Bermuda seed,
And copters rescue calves from swampy inclines,
But still, we have cowboys. Maybe the best of the breed.

For postholes, a digger by hand is not what you need.
A power takeoff can scoop it, in rain or shine.
Remember the day when the land had a simpler creed?

On the Wind River Range, the burning sun will speed,
And a lingering "Kee!" calls cattle out of the pines.
We still have cowboys. Maybe the best of the breed.

It costs a bundle for wire-bound hay to feed
A load of livestock, if sadly the rain cloud resigns.
Remember the day when the land had a simpler creed?

They tug barbed wire over rugged jimson weed.
They herd the cows to the creek with a winding lead.
We still have cowboys. Maybe the best of the breed.
Remember the day when the land had a simpler creed?

VICIOUS DUMB CRIMINALS

Where do they come from, the phrases describing the guys
Committing the kinds of crimes we see today?
The vicious, the greedy, the foolish, the just plain unwise?

Words like "registered gang members" take the prize.
If the crooks don't register, what's the fine they pay?
And where do they come from, the phrases describing these guys?

Shoplifting pros stuff goods under threads for disguise.
They hang it so heavy, it's hard to "lift" their prey.
The vicious, the greedy, the foolish, the just plain unwise.

Road rage? In recent years, it's been on the rise,
And now it's all the rage, you'd have to say.
Where do they come from, the phrases describing these guys?

Folks rob banks and escape by bike or bus.
The dumbest leave prints: a treacherous expose'.
The vicious, the greedy, the foolish, the just plain unwise.

A guy on bond? He'll give reoffending some tries,
And maybe arrange that a total stranger dies.
Where do they come from, the phrases describing these guys,
The vicious, the greedy, the foolish, the just plain unwise?

PHYSICAL THERAPY

She pulls my foot up. Keep it straight! It'll hurt.
And what was the crime I did to deserve all this?
My rubberized body's already gone inert.

Now, lift away from the chair. Touch lightly. Curt
And clear commands. The chair is like an abyss.
She pulls my foot up. Keep it straight! It'll hurt.

Next, let's see you balance, so stay alert,
With one foot behind. Now, toe this precipice.
My rubberized body's already gone inert.

Hang your leg down. Pull it straight and pert.
Right here, I want to ask for an armistice.
She pulls my foot up. Keep it straight! It'll hurt.

So now, pretend you're rolling around in dirt,
And arch your back so the table isn't kissed.
My rubberized body's already gone inert.

It'll make me better? It sounds kind of hit-or-miss.
So, where's my promised meta-morpho-sis?
She pulls my foot up. Keep it straight! It'll hurt.
My rubberized body's already gone inert.

MOVING DAY

Moving Day is coming on too fast,
With stuff wrapped up in bundles, over there,
And every box looks way too tired to last.

And where will I ever arrive, I hazily ask?
Today I wouldn't want to pay the fare,
But Moving Day is coming on too fast.

I don't know the timing. All my stories are cast
In corrugated cardboard, hardly an inch to spare,
And every box looks way too tired to last.

Books are in one container. Longtime past
Depictions of baseball heroics sit in a chair.
Moving Day is coming on too fast.

Throwaways fill a bag. Wisdom is classed
With useless Wealth, so both are packed as a pair,
And every box looks way too tired to last.

The journey disturbs the bones. My blood is harassed.
My breath is breaking and running I don't know where.
Moving Day is coming on too fast.
And every box looks way too tired to last.

SILLY SAM: HERE'S ONE FOR THE KIDS

Silly Sam, he gets confused a lot.
He carelessly thrashes his hammer to nail in a screw.
He's all mixed up. Mistakes are all he's got.

He sailed his coffee, then he drank his yacht.
He kissed the lawn, then watered his family crew.
Silly Sam, he gets confused a lot.

He drove to work in the news and read a spot
On his car. The sky was asphalt; the road was blue.
He's all mixed up. Mistakes are all he's got.

He went to sleep on his bank; drew money from his cot.
He ate his jacket for dinner while wearing some stew.
Silly Sam, he gets confused a lot.

He walked through the shades and pulled down the door to blot
The sun. He read some birds while his library flew.
He's all mixed up. Mistakes are all he's got.

He's always the target of jokes but has no clue.
He can't tell vegetable soup from library glue.
Silly Sam, he gets confused a lot.
He's all mixed up. Mistakes are all he's got.

THE GOOD AND THE BAD DONALD TRUMP

*Almighty God . . . [s]ometimes allows the mind
of a man of distinguished birth to follow its bent . . .
He permits him to lord it in many lands until the man
in his unthinkingness forgets that it will ever
end for him.*
--from Beowulf, about a thousand years ago,
   lines 1727-34 (Heaney tr.)

He did some wonderful things, supporters are sure.
He boosted the national military might,
But his sense of propriety couldn't seem to endure.

He raised the economy. Those who collected more
Were the needy, who gained the greatest height.
He did some wonderful things, supporters are sure.

He claimed the election was stolen, tried to secure
The outcome with frivolous lawsuits he wanted to fight.
His sense of propriety couldn't seem to endure.

There came a pandemic. A desperate need for a cure.
His Warp Speed mission brought the end in sight.
He did some wonderful things, supporters are sure.

He made the southern border more secure,
But the mob that invaded the Senate was his to invite.
His sense of propriety couldn't seem to endure.

Now his endorsements, for reasons sometimes obscure,
Find losers more than winners, and in spite
Of his having done wonderful things, supporters are sure,
His sense of propriety couldn't seem to endure.

DEATH ROW FABLES

I didn't do it. The rap on me was a frame.
The next guy killed three kids on LSD.
We all did something, but all of you share the blame.

They say I robbed and slashed this fancy dame.
I've filed my writs. I bet I'll soon go free.
I didn't do it. The rap on me was a frame.

Down the way, that famous what's-his-name
Is just a butcher, far as I can see.
We all did something, but all of you share the blame.

This guy's thrown his garbage at whoever came.
He hops and screams at night like a chimpanzee.
But I didn't do it. The rap on me was a frame.

That one there is a nightmare. Got no shame.
Sadistic. But heck, not guilty is still his plea.
We all did something, but all of you share the blame.

They say I did it, but guilt is no one's game,
And looking out there, you're just as guilty as me.
I didn't do it. The rap on me was a frame.
We all did something, but all of you share the blame.

Great Villanelles of the Past

The greatest villanelle ever written is Dylan Thomas's ***Do Not Go Gentle into That Good Night.*** His message is that life is precious. Thomas's father is dying, and he urges him to fight against the progress of death. His first and third lines, "Do not go gentle into that good night," and "Rage, rage against the dying of the light," make powerful repetitions throughout the poem. It's well worth looking up, just with the words "Do not go gentle."

Here's how it starts:

> Do not go gentle into that good night,
> Old age should burn and rave at close of day;
> Rage, rage against the dying of the light.

I'm not trying to compete with Thomas. I don't think anyone will do that for years to come.

The second-best villanelle, according to that noted expert, me, is Sylvia Plath's ***Mad Girl's Love Song.*** Sylvia speaks to an imaginary man who has left her. The first and third lines, "I close my eyes and all the world drops dead" and "I think I made you up inside my head," show the girl's madness, which reaches a high point with:

> I fancied you'd return the way you said,
> But I grow old and I forget your name.
> (I think I made you up inside my head.)

Dylan Thomas drank himself to death. Sylvia Plath tried repeatedly to commit suicide and finally, after years of attempts, succeeded in killing herself. I hope this pattern doesn't extend to all of us villanelle writers.

NEW HOME PURCHASE

You'd almost like to ignore them and not call back,
But it's too much money. It's also where home will be,
And any detail can throw the deal off track.

You find out, this doctor, the seller, is really a quack.
The guy gets drunk every day around two or three.
You'd almost like to ignore them and not call back.

Still worse, his broker keeps mice in her haversack.
She stops twice a day to talk to her willow tree.
And any detail can throw the deal off track.

Your seller wants to end up in the black.
You're paying top dollar, but he says you're getting it free.
You'd almost like to ignore them and not call back.

Your lender's decided the interest is out of whack.
He says he'll increase it by just a tiny degree,
And any detail can throw the deal off track.

Then, when anger is forcing the contract to crack,
You give away something small and it clears the debris.
The deal gets done. Ignore them and don't call back.
Forget the details that could have thrown it off track.

THE ISLAMIC REPUBLIC OF IRAN

Mayhem follows the flag with the red and green bar.
The ayatollahs' fatwas decree who'll die.
It's all religion, including nuclear war.

They like the damage done by a bomb in a car.
They chant the deathly jihadist battle cry.
Mayhem follows the flag with the red and green bar.

America wants a treaty, and that's bizarre:
Iranians hide their crimes, and they know how to lie.
It's all religion, including nuclear war.

A martyr who kills on American soil is an avatar
And bound for heaven. His fame is forever high,
And mayhem follows the flag with the red and green bar.

They kill noncombatants with cannons that fire from afar.
They shout that every Israeli ought to die.
It's all religion, including nuclear war.

Agreements with this kind of misfits aren't worth a dinar.
The mullahs want a bomb, and here is why.
Mayhem follows the flag with the red and green bar.
It's all religion, including nuclear war.

ANDERSON STREET VILLANELLE

I happened to watch it all on Anderson Street:
An elephant roughed up a covey of purple apes.
I saw two light waves slow and stop, then meet.

An octopus flew from town to find something to eat,
And a seaplane landed with pilots in rubberized capes.
I happened to watch it all on Anderson Street.

There also was this: Houdini bowed to greet
The Dalai Lama, who sported his fanciest drapes.
I saw two light waves slow and stop, then meet.

Lincoln gave his address. Little Leaguers beat
The New York Yankees. They played near a grotto of grapes.
I happened to watch it all on Anderson Street.

But *you* don't believe me? With lots of snow and sleet,
For sure, I can prove it! Just look at my videotapes.
See, *there's* the snow! Where you see the light waves meet.

McDonald's was serving gourmet strawberry crepes,
And Elvis was singing with spangles that shifted their shapes.
I happened to watch it all on Anderson Street,
When I saw two light waves slow and stop, then meet.

EMAILS

I get too many messages every day.
Senders change addresses. I can't get them gone,
And most of my emails need to get washed away.

For instance, I get these unwanted ads that say,
"We'll teach you real estate without a yawn!"
I get too many messages every day.

Emails selling brands of mosquito spray
Or a homesite that features a beautiful, golden dawn:
Most of my emails need to get washed away.

Emails selling relief from the taxes I pay.
Emails selling a greener, healthier lawn.
I get too many messages every day.

Emails offering gambling sites to play
And emails offering loans for whatever I pawn.
Most of my emails need to get washed away.

I've got to read them. Some are my work display.
As fast as I erase, they're coming on.
I get too many messages every day,
And most of my emails need to be washed away.

SENTINEL

My dictionary, I swear it's watching me,
The kind that's a great big volume and spreads on a rack.
It's open and holds all the words that are fit to see.

"Instinct" follows "impropriety"
In here, and "avarice" follows "amnesiac."
My dictionary, I swear it's watching me.

It gives you examples: say, for "analogy,"
"The earth is like a ball"; "a nail's like a tack."
It's open and holds all the words that are fit to see.

It tells where they come from; words like "prosody,"
From Latin.* How many secrets can this book unpack?
My dictionary, I swear it's watching me.

What's "paranoid?" "You, thinking you're watched by me":
That's written but hidden? Somewhere, in white and black?
It's open and holds all the words that are fit to see.

There's all this obscure and dizzy philosophy.
You're mesmerized, and your memory wanders free . . .
Maybe that's why . . . I swear, it's watching me.
It's open and holds all the words that are fit to see.

---

*Which is defined as "That part of grammar treating . . . the laws of versification," such as the rules governing this villanelle.

WORLD SERIES 2022: THE HOUSTON POINT OF VIEW

It's fun when the hometown team can manage a win,
Like the great World Series of twenty twenty-two.
Psychologists say we should carry a happy grin.

Game *one* broke all of Houston's breathing, when
The Phillies hit home runs, and more than a few.
Not fun, when the hometown team can't manage a win.

The pitching returned at last and was able to skin
The Phillies with screaming sliders in number *two.*
Psychologists say we should carry a happy grin.

The Astros flew to Philadelphia, then,
But they lost game *three* and it looked as though they were through.
Not fun, when the hometown team can't manage a win.

Game *four* was a whole lot better than where we'd been:
That no-hitter took us four different pitchers to do.
Psychologists say we should carry a happy grin.

We won game *five* by a run: a scare to the end.
We won the *last* with a long ball that sailed and flew.
It's fun when the hometown team can manage a win.
Psychologists say we should carry a happy grin.

WAKING UP AT FOUR A.M.

My teeth were shaking when I pushed my legs out of bed
At four o'clock. The night was as dark as coal.
It's early, but I just couldn't sleep, and my feet were like lead.

I don't want to wake the whole house. I stumble, instead,
To pull on some clothes, and I hear the hour toll.
My teeth were shaking when I pushed my legs out of bed.

I watch the stairs, so as not to fall on my head.
I slam back coffee. I cram a cinnamon roll.
It's early, but I just couldn't sleep, and my feet are like lead.

I let the dogs out. I get the headlines read
But not the rest of the paper. I watch the TV scroll.
My teeth were shaking when I pushed my legs out of bed.

Meds and drops come next. My eyes are red,
But now I can see. My desk is a papered-up bowl.
It's early but I just couldn't sleep, and my feet are like lead.

In a couple of hours I'll leave, no longer half-dead,
For the office and there, I'll make up the sleep I stole.
My teeth were shaking when I pushed my legs out of bed
Too early, but I just couldn't sleep, and my feet were like lead.

AUSTIN, TEXAS

Austin, Texas, is branching like a vine
In all directions. Cranes sprout everywhere.
It's a little blue spot in a state with a solid red line.

The traffic's like New York City. You hear the whine
Of gaseous trucks from the valley roughen the air.
Austin, Texas, is branching like a vine.

The interstate spins it a hardened concrete spine,
But its woken custom encourages weirdness with flair,
This little blue spot in a state with a solid red line.

Devices made of keys and clicks combine
In products that use them for music and medical care.
Austin, Texas, is branching like a vine.

Towers blanket downtown. They wink and shine
Up in the hills at night, a show to share.
It's a little blue spot in a state with a solid red line.

The limestone capitol dome is featured fine
As the focus of Congress Avenue's busy design.
Austin, Texas, is branching like a vine:
A little blue spot in a state with a solid red line.

EDGAR ALLAN POE

> *True! Nervous—very, very dreadfully nervous I have been, and am! But why <u>will</u> you say I am mad? . . . I heard all things in heaven and in the earth. I heard many things in hell. How, then, am I mad?*
> Edgar Allan Poe, *The Tell-Tale Heart* (1843)

He writes short stories, always a twist at the end,
Except that with Poe, there's usually someone who dies,
And horror and darkness were all he could comprehend.

The Black Cat invents a narrator who will send
His wife inside a wall, but the law will find a surprise.
He writes short stories: always a twist at the end.

The Tell-Tale Heart sees a similar hero extend
His madness to murder and hide behind casual lies.
Horror and darkness were all he could comprehend.

With *The Murders in the Rue Morgue*, Poe would extend
The first detective adventure to modern eyes.
He writes short stories: always a twist at the end.

He never knew that *The Raven* would finally lend
Its name when football in Baltimore would arise.
Horror and darkness were all he could comprehend.

His strange imaginings happily would analyze
Insane assassins and crimes they tried to disguise.
He writes short stories: always a twist at the end,
But horror and darkness were all he could comprehend.

SHOPGIRL

She hears the alarm at five and catches the bus,
And then another bus, to get there at eight.
It's a job at the knickknacks counter. Not much to discuss.

At nine, it opens. A customer raises a fuss
At the shopgirl. The reason: a string isn't straight.
She hears the alarm at five and catches the bus.

It's nine bucks an hour, and hearing this woman cuss
Isn't worth it. But she's got to listen, even to hate.
It's a job at the knickknacks counter. Not much to discuss.

Can't sit. Got to stand. Good makeup and dress are a must.
Lunchtime means rest, but a purchase keeps her late.
She hears the alarm at five and catches the bus.

Then three straight returns. One is full of dust
And requires the boss. And he becomes irate.
It's a job at the knickknacks counter. Not much to discuss.

At five, she's held over. Two buses home aren't great,
And she wishes that others just knew her weary state.
She hears the alarm at five and catches the bus.
It's a job at the knickknacks counter. Not much to discuss.

CROSSWORD PUZZLES

How do they write these things? I often say.
How do they get the "downs" and "acrosses" to work?
For crossword makers, I guess I'm easy prey.

The New York Times example is like, "No way."
Does each clue really hide answers that somewhere lurk?
How do they write these things? I often say.

Can't get the across. And next, to the down I stray.
Can't get that one either. I need a clever clerk.
For crossword makers, I guess I'm easy prey.

At last, I may have sixteen-down. A ray
Of hope. But it's wrong. Is it written just to irk?
How do they write these things? I often say.

I can't guess anything else. I'm through for today.
It makes me mad. The writer of this is a jerk.
For crossword makers, I guess I'm easy prey.

So, should I try something easier? Well, it may
Turn out, I can't do that one, either. My edges would fray.
How do they write these things? I often say.
For crossword makers, I guess, I'm easy prey.

My Own Rules for a Villanelle
(Not exactly commandments, but this is what I try to do)

1. Natural-sounding lines, with normal words. Including informal speech, when appropriate. Not flowery words. (Mostly.)

2. No inverted sentences. Some poets turn their lines upside down to fit the rhyme. Although . . . a few lines in here are inverted. For example, in the next poem, "The wisdom of the past, you shouldn't blithely betray." Oh, well. Poetic license.

3. Get the meaning across first, then worry about the rhyme. It's hard, but it makes a better poem. It's advice from Donald Mace Williams, a wonderful writer, although I don't express it as well as he does.

4. Vary the rhyme if it works better, especially in the last four lines. The traditional pattern for that stanza is ABAA. It often sounds better as BBAA.

5. All kinds of subjects, from love to weather to just plain fun with words. But some of the subjects here are rough, such as death row or Iran.

6. Irreverence, when it works. The next villanelle, for instance, challenges greatness. A famous poem gives bad advice, even though it's a remarkable work.

7. Tap out each line to make sure of the meter. Also from Mr. Williams.

8. The usual literary devices. Irony. Symbolism. Analogy. Suggestion, Ambiguity. Alliteration. Internal rhyme. Etc., etc.

9. Search for the perfect word. Today, we have resources that writers of the past didn't, such as thesaurus.com and rhymer.com. Keep looking for the right word.

A YELLOW WOOD AND BAD ADVICE

> *Two roads diverged in a wood, and I—*
> *I took the one less traveled by,*
> *And that has made all the difference.*
>   --Robert Frost

The poet's roads diverged in a yellow wood,
And he chose the surly, overgrown, wilder way:
Advice that mostly isn't very good.*

It seemed like a decent idea, at first. He could
Have discovered wealth or at least had a fun kind of day,
The poet whose roads diverged in a yellow wood.

But his avenue narrows to nothing. A towering flood
Has ripped the ravine. He's heard somebody say
A word of advice that mostly wasn't good.

He breaks into brambles. They crack and bruise his hood
And then his head, while the rain goes grimy and gray,
The poet whose roads diverged in a yellow wood.

His plan depended on paths that deepened. He should
Have had shadowing oaks and luck that lasted his stay—
Or avoided advice that wasn't very good.

The wisdom of the past, you shouldn't blithely betray.
Romantic choices don't tell where the path once lay.
The poet whose roads diverged in a yellow wood
Provides advice that mostly isn't good.

---

*Actually, the poem is complex. It might be about regret at taking the wrong path. It might even be the musings of an old man (signified by the yellow wood).

A QUEEN FOR AMERICA

Why doesn't America crown our very own queen,
To greet the guests with sideways waves of her hand?*
The people would watch her, but she'd be squeaky clean.

She'd act American, more so than anyone's seen.
She'd drink only bourbon, not scotch, and travel the land.
Why doesn't America crown our very own queen?

She'd start the race at Daytona. She'd fill up the screen
At the next World Series and fling the ball from the stands.
The people would watch her, but she'd be squeaky clean.

Her royal highness would dress up on Halloween,
Perhaps as a princess. She'd listen to indie bands.
Why doesn't America crown our very own queen?

She'd paint it pink, her armored limousine.
She'd sport proper beachwear to wiggle her toes in the sand.
The people would watch her, but she'd be squeaky clean.

She'd glare at the Federal Reserve but still stay serene.
She'd sail an aircraft carrier under her command.
Why doesn't America crown our very own queen?
The people would watch her, but she'd be squeaky clean.

---

*We can't. It would be unconstitutional. Article I, Section 9, Clause 8 says, "No title of nobility shall be granted by the United States."

GRAB THE DAY

It's rainy season, but clouds are cordial today.
They bring on a dozen ideas about what to do,
And you've got to pursue them while doubting the proper way.

Foolish mortals model their futures in clay,
Completely planned, when the purpose is only a clue.
It's rainy season, but clouds are cordial today.

Wiser people played it where it lay,
In the rough or the fairway, forgetting an error or two.
You've got to pursue it while doubting the proper way.

Horatius said, forget the future, grab the day.*
This is the only time when life is new.
It's rainy season, but clouds are cordial today.

If you see in the wind a forking sunlight ray,
It's a signal that great good fortune is searching for you.
You've got to pursue it while doubting the proper way.

So live in this moment, with skies no longer gray.
Don't wait for dreams of grandeur. They never come true.
It's rainy season, but clouds are cordial today.
You've got to pursue it while doubting the proper way.

---

*Usually, it's "seize the day," but that's bad translation. The Latin is more like "pluck the day," like plucking a flower, but that sounds silly. "Grab the day" is more like it, maybe.

A VILLANELLE SHOVED TOGETHER OUT OF SEVERAL REALLY OLD AND TIRED JOKES

There's verbiage here that's less than mesmerizing.
"A termite walks in a bar and asks, 'Where's the bar tender?'" *
It's that kind of nonsense these stanzas are emphasizing.

"Waiter, this fly in my soup is unappetizing."
"So? The chef was a tailor: a trousers mender."
There's verbiage here that's less than mesmerizing.

"What did one flea say to another after arising?"
"Shall we walk, or shall we take the dog?" Remember,
It's that kind of nonsense these stanzas are emphasizing.

"What was the cave-man writing teacher centralizing?"
"Structure your drawings better! Structure makes splendor!"
There's verbiage here that's less than mesmerizing.

"Why was an ant, while crossing a carton, mobilizing?"
"It says to tear on the dotted line!" replied the contender.
It's that kind of nonsense these stanzas are emphasizing.

The shrink says, "You're crazy." His patient, agonizing:
"A second opinion?" "Okay. You're not exactly slender!"
There's verbiage here that's less than mesmerizing.
It's that kind of nonsense these stanzas are emphasizing.

---

*Some people don't get this one. Hey, he's a termite! And what is the bar made of?

THE XANADU DOME

In Xanadu did Kubla Khan
A stately pleasure-dome decree
Where Alph, the sacred river, ran
Through caverns measureless to man
Down to a sunless sea.
   —Samuel Taylor Coleridge

In a strange sort of dream, I chanced to gaze upon
A bright green river surrounding a castle gate:
The stately pleasure dome of Kubla Khan!

The windows were diamonds, with frames as white as bone.
The doors were princely; the roof was perfect slate,
In the strange sort of dream that I chanced to gaze upon.

A glistening fountain with orchids, a gliding swan,
And a stable of horses with even, thundering gait:
The stately pleasure dome of Kubla Khan.

And now, here is Kubla himself! As bright as the sun,
Beside his queen, he cavorts in a gleeful state,
In the strange sort of dream that I chanced to gaze upon.

Carpets of gold covered floors of obsidian,
And servants in stark white tunics stood sharply straight,
In the stately pleasure dome of Kubla Khan.

But suddenly then, the castle walls were none
And I awakened. My vision blurred and was gone.
In a strange sort of dream, I'd chanced to gaze upon
The stately pleasure dome of Kubla Khan!

ELVIS

He worked with the greatest gimmick a star could bring,
Surprising, maybe, to many of us in the crowd,
But it wasn't his suits or sideburns. Elvis could sing.

He started with gospel, and you always heard it ring
Like hallelujahs, even when the song wasn't loud.
He worked with the greatest gimmick a star could bring.

His older songs were shouted, like bouncing bling,
And then more tender, like a whispered cloud.
It wasn't his suits or sideburns. Elvis could sing.

Sometimes he borrowed, but always he would cling
To his roots, where Tennessee rock 'n roll ran proud.
He worked with the greatest gimmick a star can bring.

In concert he twisted and turned like a wound-up spring
And shook so much, the groupies screamed and wowed.
It wasn't his suits or sideburns. Elvis could sing.

He left us too soon, but no one's challenging
His legend, his magic. He'll always be the king.
He had the greatest gimmick a star could bring,
But it wasn't his suits or sideburns. Elvis could sing.

NEW HOUSTON VISITOR

"Near the airport, this city is lush and green,"
He thought to himself. "Can this be Houston I see?
"I expected cactus, horses, and a desert scene!"

The downtown towers guide a fuel machine
Discovering energy out of the farthest sea,
And everywhere, this city is lush and green.

Southward, massive medical crews will convene
For dozens of transplants a week, rejection-free.
"But I expected cactus, horses, and a desert scene!"

To the east, the spacecraft center lies between
The bay and the town, designing ships for apogee,
And everywhere, the city is lush and green.

Westward, the streets don't resemble the byzantine
Designs back east. They glide to meadows and trees.
"But I expected cactus, horses and a desert scene!"

The Opera House is lovely, and all can agree,
Performances are truly amazing to see.
"And everywhere, the city is lush and green,
"But I expected cactus, horses and a desert scene!"

COVID

He's even been socked with his boosters. He ought to be clear.
He's sometimes, at least, been living sort of right.
He's also avoided people in groups for a year.

But now he's crammed with Covid. Why? We hear
It can happen. Maybe he partied too much last night?
He's even been stabbed with his boosters. He ought to be clear.

He feels just crummy. He's mauled all the way from his ear
To his feet. He's way too drained to be dragged to this fight.
He's even avoided people in groups for a year.

He's a member of a delicate group where fear
Of serious consequences isn't so slight.
He's even been stuck with his boosters. He ought to be clear.

His throat is crawling. His eyes and mouth appear
To be dripping rainbows. His head is rippling and tight.
He's even avoided people in groups for a year.

Aw, what the heck! he reasons. He reckons he might
As well have a raucous time and drink some beer.
Why'd he get stabbed with his boosters? He ought to be clear.
And why's he avoided people in groups for a year?

ALWAYS, FOREVER REAL

My love for you will always, forever be real.
I trust my hand to you and only you,
A promise to keep, with a heart as sturdy as steel.

I'll make your coffee. I'll earn the money. To seal
The deal, I'll make the bed on occasion, too.
My love for you will always, forever be real.

On every birthday, I'll work to make you feel
Like a star. In fact, that's what I'll constantly do.
A promise to keep, with a heart as sturdy as steel

We'll fly to Florence and visit the haughty appeal
Of Michelangelo's David and walk the gallery through.
My love for you will always, forever be real.

I'll gather you diamonds and gold but only reveal
These baubles at times that soar with surprises for you.
A promise to keep, with a heart as sturdy as steel.

I'll bring you a thousand flowers tied in blue-
And-gold bows, and songs of joy like magic, but true.
My love for you will always, forever be real:
A promise to keep, with a heart as sturdy as steel.

RETIRE? BUT WHAT WILL YOU DO?

Voices tell you, retire. But should you obey?
"Two or three years, and then it ought to be time."
But what will you do, day after day after day?

Get a hobby? That's what people say.
You've already got a couple, like reading this rhyme.
Voices tell you, retire. But should you obey?

Work less at your usual calling? Or else heave hay,
Except that your strength wouldn't even be worth a dime.
So, what will you do, day after day after day?

Or find a nonprofit. Watch kids squashing clay
Into figures? Hospital visits? Combating crime?
Voices tell you, retire. But should you obey?

They know you've lost a step and you're edging toward gray,
And they're thinking of you; but it doesn't manage the climb
You're considering: what will you do, day after day?

They're right; there will come a time not far away
When you won't fake it as well in the role you play.
Voices tell you, retire. But should you obey?
And what will you do, day after day after day?

SEMIOTICS, METAPHYSICS, AND THE COLOR CALLED "RED"

Plato's forms were shown in a cave on the wall,
But blurry. And what is "red" but a slippery mass
Of colors merged and blended into a ball?

Beauty and justice, abstractions your finger might scrawl,
Can't capture what semiotics, the science of symbols,* lets last.
Plato's forms were shown in a cave on the wall.

And one person's red is not another's at all.
Shakespeare asked us, what's in a name to hold fast?
Just colors merged and blended into a ball.

And is there a shade so that metaphysics** would call
It red? The gulf between word and wavelength is vast.
Plato's forms were shown in a cave on the wall.

And what can anyone know of just how small
Our colorless universe was, and why it passed
Toward colors merged and blended into a ball?

So, no one can find an easy protocol
For major ideas. They're visions: a color blast.
Plato's forms were shown in a cave on the wall,
In colors merged and blended into a ball.

---

*Semiotics is the study of symbols, including words, and how they are perceived.
**Metaphysics is said to consider the "most fundamental" questions, such as the nature of reality.

DOGS

We love our dogs, love every single one,
Even the ones that make trouble, the ones that get lost.
They're unpredictable. That's what makes them fun.

Shepherds want to get wet in the surf and run.
Beagles circle around so the leash gets crossed.
We love our dogs, love every single one.

Labs are loyal until their lives are gone.
They love you fiercely, and yet they can't be bossed.
They're unpredictable. That's what makes them fun.

Collies like to wrestle until they're done.
Retrievers run after cars and don't care about exhaust.
We love our dogs, love every single one.

They'll tear their toys up, into oblivion,
And none of them thinks about what those playthings cost.
They're unpredictable. That's what makes them fun.

They'll bug you to death about a jerky bone.
They'll bug you to death until that ball gets tossed.
We love our dogs, love every single one.
They're unpredictable. That's what makes them fun!

TRUTH

What is truth? said jesting Pilate, and would
Not stay for an answer.* Truth is a quick auctioneer,
And whatever you think is true. You've done what you could.

Truth is experiment. Results are good
If they're proved by tests. Would you say then, the truth will appear?
What is truth? said jesting Pilate, and would.

Truth is coded. Gravity holds you, but should
The reason be this, or that, if it pleases the ear?
Whatever you think is true. You've done what you could.

In numbers, base two, would you have understood,
That 2 + 2 isn't 4?** It isn't, here.
What is truth? said jesting Pilate, and would.

Faith is truth, as well. The likelihood
Of proof is never. But truth can make itself clear.
Whatever you think is true. You've done what you could.

Truth is what we agree in a killing flood:
If it isn't true, let's let it disappear.
What is truth? said jesting Pilate, and would.
Whatever you think is true. You've done what you could.

---

*Quoted from line 1 of Sir Francis Bacon's essay, *Of Truth*.
**There's no "2" in base 2. Counting is 1, 10, 11, 100. So, 10 (which is 2) + 10 (2) = 100 (4). That's the truth.

CARGO FROM HOUSTON

Powerful cities with charm, in wonderful lands,
Ship cargo over the world, but which one is best?
Is Houston a city fulfilling all your demands?

An elegant ship leaves France, where Paris stands
For the world of fashion, perfumes, and cuisine with zest:
A powerful city with charm in wonderful lands.

A Japanese liner carries Tokyo's brands
Of phones, devices, and autos, by Buddha blessed,
But is Houston a city fulfilling all your demands?

London's insurers and lenders ship commands
And wealth throughout the world on an empire's quest:
A powerful city with charm in wonderful lands.

South Africa's shining ocean freighter has plans
To carry gold and diamonds to points in the west.
But is Houston a city fulfilling all your demands?

An ugly, grimy tanker from Houston invests
In medicine, energy, culture, surprising the rest.
A powerful city with charm in wonderful lands,
Houston's a city fulfilling all your demands.

LAKE HOUSE

You've got to take care with a home that's on the lake.
There sure are a lot of animals hiding inside,
But the water is wonderful here where the cottonwoods break.

Open the window at morning when first you wake
And you might hear a reptile's watery, splashing slide.
You've got to take care with a home that's on the lake.

Later that day, you'll see a duck and a drake
And a bobcat fishing along the shallow side.
The water is wonderful here where the cottonwoods break.

There must be a hundred different species of snake,
Including water moccasins, bona fide.
You've got to take care with a home that's on the lake.

They say one sparrow does not a summer make,
But here's one in front with a crowd along for the ride.
The water is wonderful here where the cottonwoods break.

The sun is low on the pond, and make no mistake,
Its setting is sure to keep you satisfied.
You've got to take care with a home that's on the lake,
But the water is wonderful here where the cottonwoods break.

YEAR'S END, 2022

Twenty-22 was a strange and dangerous year.
It began on the 6th with the capitol insurrection,
And ended without any safety or peace coming near.

Then Putin's bullets and bombs went flying; but mere,
Unguarded Ukraine built robust homeland protection.
Twenty-22 was a strange and dangerous year.

Lasting inflation was everywhere brutally here,
But Congress still spent as if money were sugared confection.
It ended without any safety or peace coming near.

Our Highest Court put abortion laws in the clear.
A small-town school suffered murderous, tragic dejection.
Twenty-22 was a strange and dangerous year.

Elections didn't bring the Republicans cheer
When Trump-backed candidates suffered vivisection.
It ended without any safety or peace coming near.

Floods in the east. The Taliban beast. Austere
And deadly drought. Iranian nuclear in gear.
Twenty-22 was a strange and dangerous year.
It ended without any safety or peace coming near.

FIRST GRADER

> *By the end of first grade, some of the things they should be able to do include . . . reading . . .*
> —Google

Daddy, why? I don't want to learn how to read.
I get a job where school isn't used at all.
I'll work where opening books is the last thing I'll need.

I talked to my teacher. She says she won't concede.
She says without reading, I can't even find the mall.
Daddy, why? I don't want to learn how to read.

I'll be a doctor and patch up patients who bleed.
I'll work at a pre-school and help little children crawl.
I'll work where opening books is the last thing I'll need.

I'll be a lawyer. With juries, I'll tearfully plead.
I'll be a bouncer and break up a barroom brawl.
Daddy, why? I don't want to learn how to read.

Well then, I'll watch peoples' dogs and tend to their feed.
But what? I'll still have to read the signs on the stall?
I'll work where opening books is the last thing I'll need.

I'll win Olympic races with super speed,
Or become a basketball player and stretch up tall.
Daddy, why? I don't want to learn how to read.
I'll work where opening books is the last thing I'll need.

FORM 1040

You can't compute your taxes yourself at all?
The pages are garbled gobbledygook, is why,
And Form Ten-Forty will make your stomach crawl.

Alternative Minimum Tax will drive you to the wall.
Qualified Business Deductions? Yours won't qualify.
You can't compute your taxes yourself at all.

Then there's the Credit for Foreign Taxes. You'll call
The IRS? Before they answer, you'll die,
And Form Ten-Forty will make your stomach crawl.

By now, what you file is about an inch or so tall.
Passive Losses Limit? You've got an alibi:
You can't compute your taxes yourself at all.

You can file an extension. Forget it until the fall.
Suspended Losses will make you want to cry.
And Form Ten-Forty will make your stomach crawl.

When you figure Capital Asset Sales, the sky
Will wobble around and you'll feel hung out to dry.
You can't compute your taxes yourself at all,
And Form Ten-Forty will make your stomach crawl.

LOSING

> *Winning isn't everything. It's the only thing.*
> --attributed (apocryphally) to legendary Coach
>   Vince Lombardi

You lose a contest. Happens every day.
But a wise man said, the triumph is everything.
Lombardi told us, winning's the only way.*

It's not a deep thought. Grace in losing will pay.
I've learned, long since, you can't have the thinnest skin.
You lose a contest. Happens every day.

I've played some games when the score got way away.
I've also made real life decisions that lost like sin.
Lombardi told us, winning's the only way.

You've lost fights where the other guy said "Hey,
I've won! You're a loser." You know how convulsed you've been.
You lose a contest. Happens every day.

You've had to forgive even jerks who spitefully spray
That kind of stuff. Could be, you forgive even when
You ought to follow Lombardi: winning's the way.

The philosophy's hard to learn, to fight to the end,
But forgive and *remember,* the times you didn't win.
You lose a contest. Happens every day.
Lombardi told us, winning's the only way.

---

*He later said that he was misunderstood. He meant, on the football
 field. You want to win throughout the game and never stop trying.

GRADUATE SCHOOL PROFESSORS

Professors aren't players. They rest on their aging degrees.
The work is done by students who started with books,
And now they do it. The professor oversees.

They watch their charges from far away. They freeze
The timid with points those fumbling decisions mistook.
Professors aren't players. They rest on their aging degrees.

They can't design buildings, discover a cure for disease,
Or translate an epic. They cover the courses they took,
But students do it. The professor oversees.

They say it's a publishing job —stuff nobody reads—
And not a teaching job; that's for training a cook.
Professors aren't players. They rest on their aging degrees.

At faculty meetings, two sides squander their time
On trivial squabbles that get these scholars hooked.
Their students do it. The professor oversees.

Often, the world of reality's answer keys
Are not where the ivory tower tells you to look.
Professors aren't players. They rest on their aging degrees.
Their students do it. The professor oversees.

YOUR WEATHERMAN, NEHEMIAH GREENE

> *Diviners use these vague generalities because their predictions are less likely to be falsified. . . The oracle-monger is more likely to be right if he says that a thing will happen than if he says when it will happen.*
> --Aristotle, *Rhetoric,* Book III, Chapter 5

I'm your weatherman, Nehemiah Greene.
You'll all get better weather because I'm here,
And I'm the best at predicting that you've ever seen.

Rain is between a hundred and zero percent on your screen,
Which means it's time to check your hurricane gear.
I'm your weatherman, Nehemiah Greene.

The mold report says follow a safe routine.
The heat in summer is probably sunny and clear,
And I'm the best at predicting that you've ever seen.

Today, I'd say, is as nice as a tambourine.
It's one of the typical days of my career,
And I'm your weatherman, Nehemiah Greene.

This just in: New Jersey is wedging between
New York and Delaware. It's shaped like an ear.
I'm the best at predicting that you've ever seen.

I try to avoid extremes, but never fear.
Rely on me whenever the weather is near.
I'm your weatherman, Nehemiah Greene,
And I'm the best at predicting that you've ever seen.

PENELOPE WAITS FOR ODYSSEUS

> *In case you don't remember the odyssey: Odysseus leaves his faithful Penelope; goes on a long trip; ties himself to a mast to avoid being bewitched by the Sirens; gets captured by a giant Cyclops; meets Circe, who turns his men into*
> *animals; and returns to find suitors for Penelope occupying his home. I'd imagine she must have been upset at times.*

I've waited and wondered but still don't have the key.
I've waited and wondered but haven't glimpsed the day,
Even with all the rage that now is me.

The man I lost is nowhere, and I can't see
When he listens to Sirens, how he'll sail away.
I've waited and wondered but still don't have the key.

A one-eyed giant will catch him. If ever he's free
In his long and holy journey, will he come my way,
Even with all the rage that now is me?

He'll also find Circe, a woman whose awful decree
Can make her visitors pigs who'll always obey.
I've waited and wondered but still don't have the key.

Elegant wastrels bid for me loathsomely.
I feel their venom bleat and burn and bray,
Even with all the rage that now is me.

To fate and madness I turn, with downward knee,
To prayer and sacrifice, all that I can pay.
I've waited and wondered but still don't have the key,
Even with all the rage that now is me.

SAILING INTO HEADWINDS

A headwind means you'll have to tack and weave
And watch when the boom begins to come around,
But you'll struggle to shore if you work your sheets and believe.

You'll need to tighten your belt, and not just grieve,
If funds at the startup you've built start coming unwound.
A headwind means you'll have to tack and weave.

Your partner's death means heartbreak. He also can't leave
Behind his wisdom. You'll hustle when the boom makes sound,
But you'll struggle to shore if you work your sheets and believe.

You lost big money when sharks set out to deceive
You, so luff your sail to windward and don't get drowned.
A headwind means you'll have to tack and weave.

When your family is falling apart, and you find no reprieve,
Watch the purple water for reefs inbound.
You'll struggle to shore if you work your sheets and believe.

A serious storm will call on you to heave
To the waves, trim sails, and keep from running aground.
A headwind means you'll have to tack and weave,
But you'll struggle to shore if you work your sheets and believe.

WORDS

A word is like the skin of a living thought.*
It pulsates transparently, breathing, but locked in a tomb.
Words are a gift that thousands of years have brought.

It started with clucks that early hominids taught
Each other, to hunt, to pray, to break a winter's gloom.
A word is like the skin of a living thought.

Most of the world didn't know that zero is naught
Till Arabic language made mathematics bloom.
Words are a gift that thousands of years have brought.

And words wrote treaties where World War II was fought,
Designed to bend so that envoys had bickering room.
A word is like the skin of a living thought.

And words make more words: A catch means that something is caught,
In the endlessly shifting shapes that speech can assume.
Words are a gift that thousands of years have brought.

Words carry greatness that all of us have sought:
Singers belt them, and drill sergeants make them boom.
A word is like the skin of a living thought,
And words are a gift that thousands of years have brought.

---

*This phrase is attributable to Oliver Wendell Holmes.